In loving memory of David Hafner.

This life is not my own,
This world is not my home,
The gospel must be known.
- KF

# CHRISTIANS AROUND THE WORLD

WRITTEN & ILLUSTRATED BY KYLE FAST

I'm sure you can think of several Christians who live in your town, city, or village.

Maybe you've seen them at church,
helping people in your community,
or taking care of a sick family member.

But did you know there are Christians all around the world? That's right! From snowy Minnesota in the USA...

...to the sunny beaches of Australia, Christians all over the globe gather in the name of Jesus to worship God!

When you lay your head down to sleep
after saying your nightly prayers...

…there are Christians on the other side of the world thanking God for a new day!

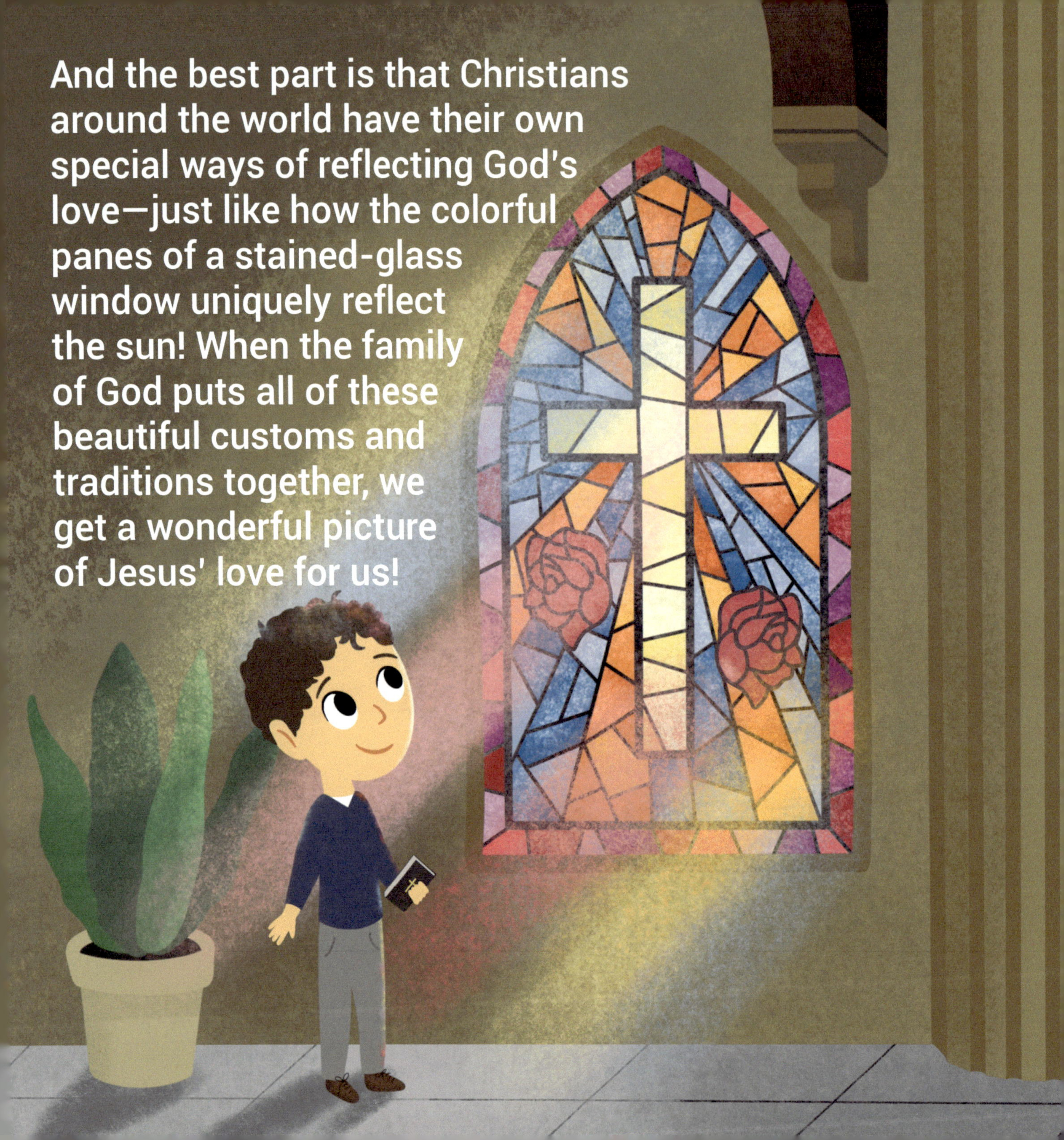

And the best part is that Christians around the world have their own special ways of reflecting God's love—just like how the colorful panes of a stained-glass window uniquely reflect the sun! When the family of God puts all of these beautiful customs and traditions together, we get a wonderful picture of Jesus' love for us!

Let's take a look at how some of God's family around His beautifully diverse world uniquely reflect the light of Jesus!

Way up in the clouds near the Himalayan Mountains, Christians in Darjeeling, India, greet one another by pressing their palms together and proudly proclaiming, *“Jai Masih!”* (say: JAY MAH-see)

*Jai Masih* means "Victory to Christ," and that in Jesus, we can have mountaintop victories over the things that make us scared or afraid. Is there anything Jesus can help you not be afraid of today?

Christians near the banks of the Rio Grande in Reynosa, Mexico, love to respond by exclaiming, *"¡Bien, gracias a Dios!"*
(say: Bee-en, grah-see-ahs ah Dee-ohs)
whenever someone asks them how they are.

The joyful response means they are doing well, thanks to God! Can you think of ways that your life is good today because of God?

Christians in Uganda love to celebrate the joy and forgiveness we have in Jesus by dancing with all their might for the Lord, just like David did in the Bible!

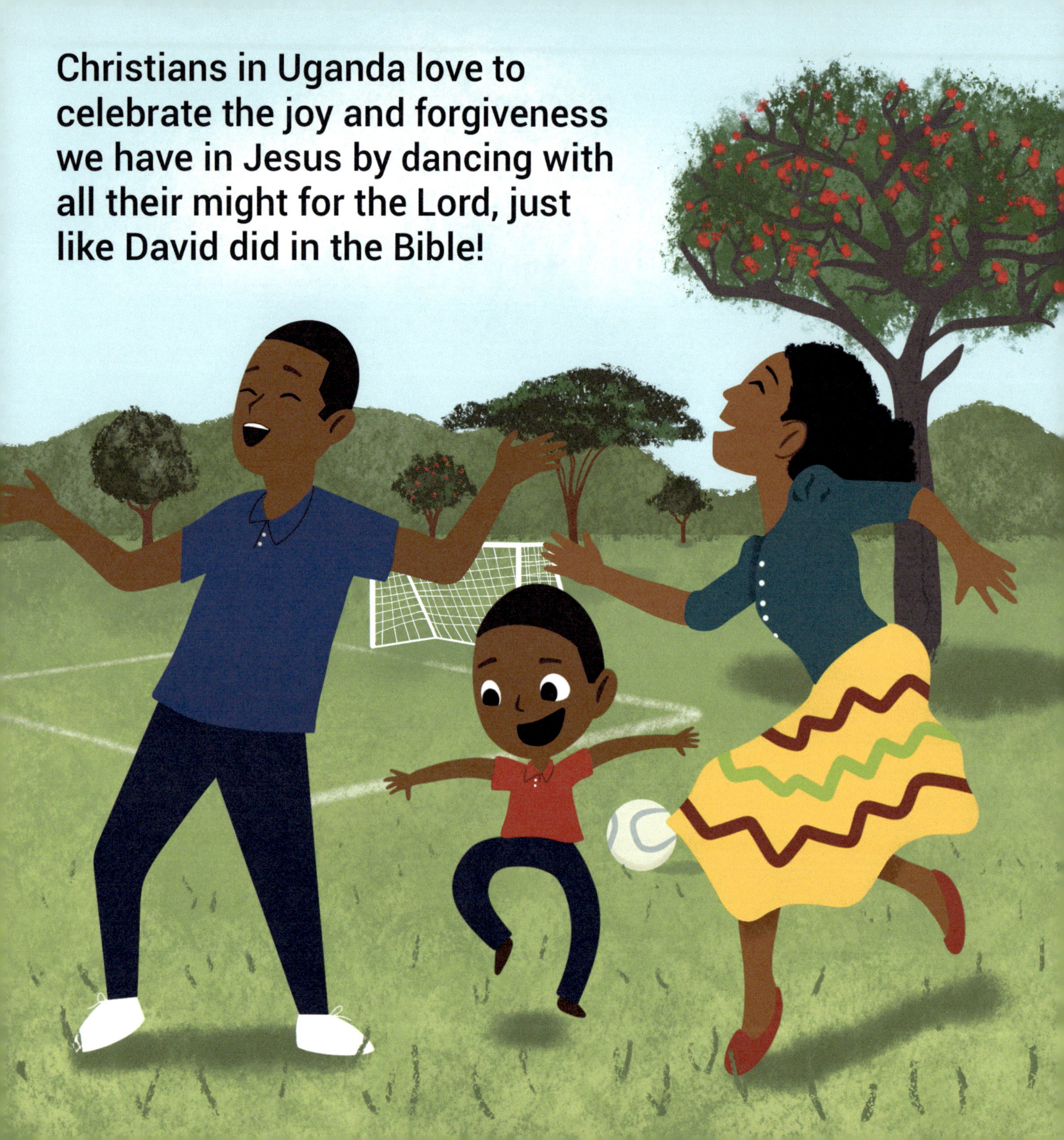

Do you have a favorite praise song?
Can you show Jesus some of your best dance moves to proclaim how thankful you are for His love?
He loves to see them!

Every spring, Christians in the United Kingdom hold daffodil festivals to admire God's beautiful creation and celebrate the miracle of Easter and new life in Jesus!

Is there anything in God's creation where you live that you think is really beautiful? Did you know that God made it just for you to enjoy?

When Christians gather in South Korea, they like to use a unique prayer style called *Tongsung Kido* (say: Tong-sung KEE-doe). In this style, everyone prays aloud together for God to help them or people in need.

Let's try this prayer style together. What did everyone pray for? Isn't it amazing that God can hear everyone's prayers perfectly and cares about the needs of so many people?

But did you know that in some places, it's actually illegal to follow Jesus and gather together for church? Christians in these places have to meet secretly—sometimes in the middle of the night—to worship together.

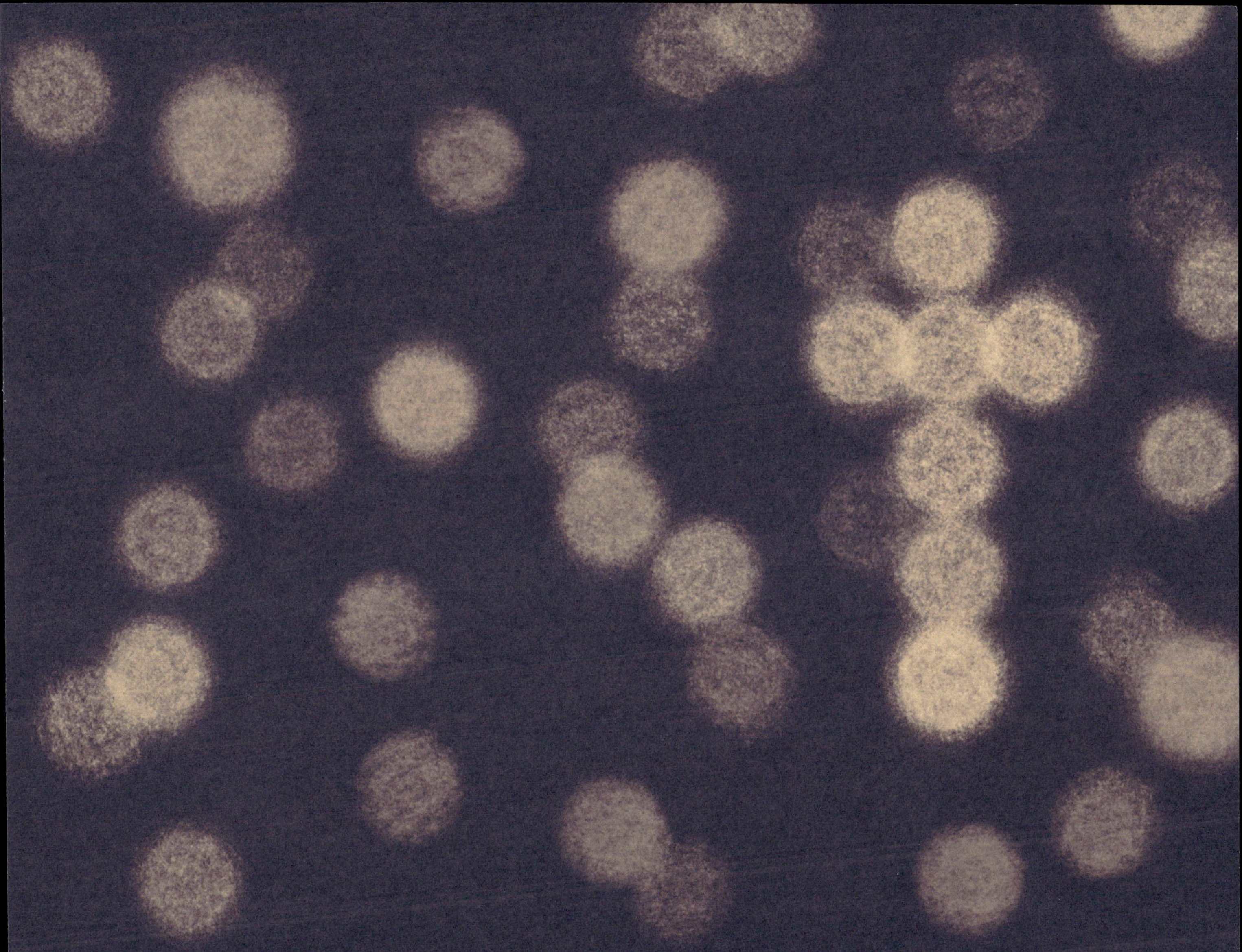

Nothing can stop the light of Jesus from shining through the darkness, though, and the number of unashamed Christians in these places is growing every year! Praise the Lord!

However, there are still many places around the world where people have never heard the name of Jesus or know a single Christian.

People in these places don't know just how much God loves them, and the rest of God's family is missing out on the ways God has uniquely made them to reflect His image—like pieces missing from a beautiful but incomplete stained-glass window.

Thankfully, the Holy Spirit is helping Christians all over the globe share the good news of Jesus with the entire world.

Many Christians are working on translating the Bible into the over 7,000 languages spoken across the globe so that everyone has access to the Word of God in their own language!

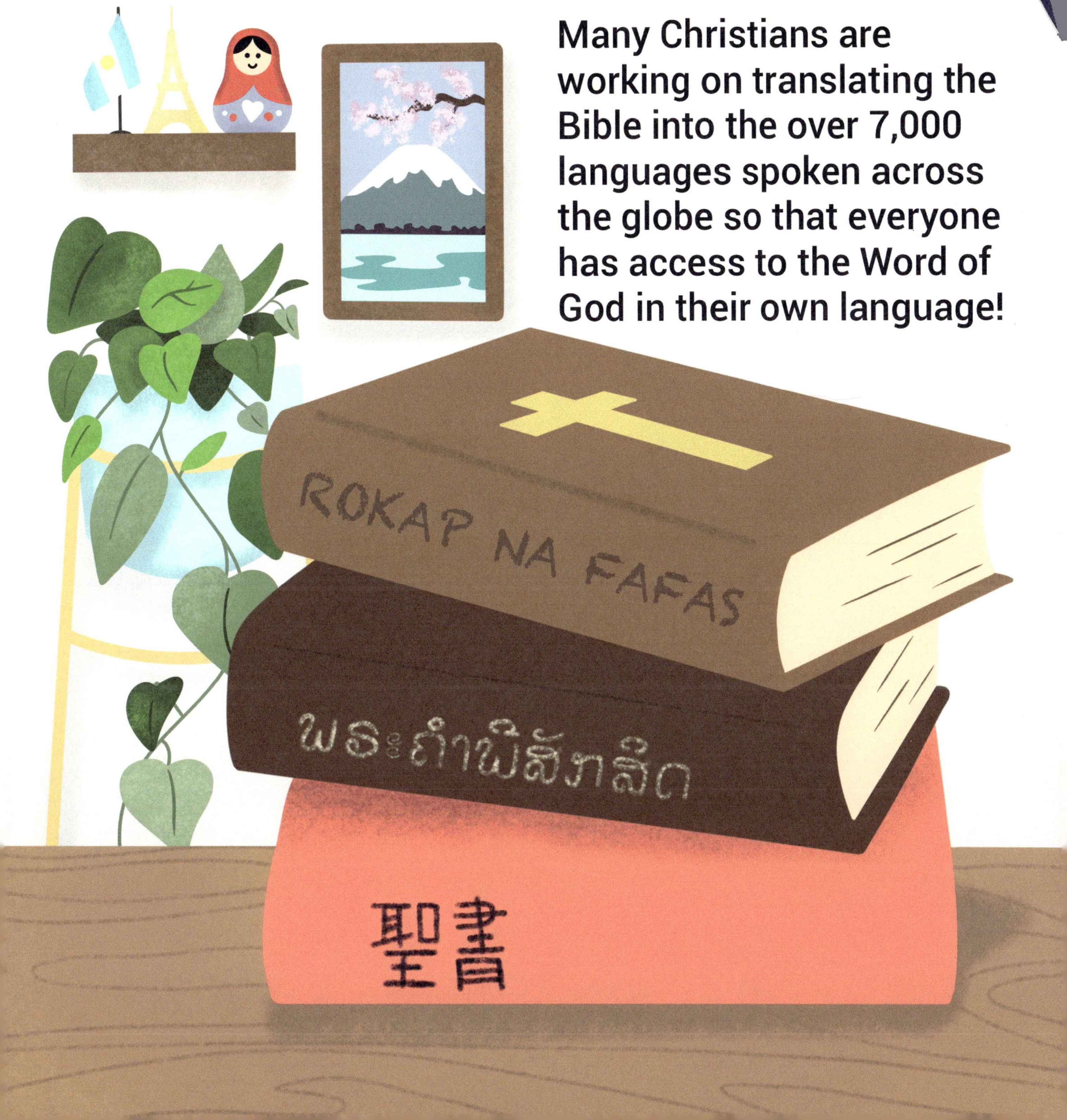

Other Christians are letting their unique lights shine before the world in many different ways!

From musicians across the world sharing the hope of Jesus to countless churches, ministries, and Spirit-filled believers spreading God's love, Christians are working together to welcome more people into God's family every day—and you can help, too!

For the Bible says that one day, people from every nation, tribe, and language will stand before the throne of God to worship the one true King in a full display of His glory and grace!

Now that you know there are Christians all around the world letting their needed and perfectly placed lights shine brightly for Jesus, isn't it encouraging to know that followers of Jesus can learn so much about God and His love from one another?

Maybe there are Christians from other parts of the world right where you live that you can get to know to learn about how they uniquely reflect the light of God!

# AUTHOR'S NOTES

Growing up in rural Southwest Minnesota, I didn't realize how big God's family of believers all around the world was until getting involved with the campus ministry Cru at Minnesota State, Mankato. Through a couple of overseas mission trips and the help of patient mentors like Dave Hafner, God opened my eyes to His heart for the nations and how I can learn so much about Him from my fellow brothers and sisters in Christ around the world. I was inspired to write *Christians Around the World* after visiting friends in Darjeeling, India, and seeing their tremendous faith in Jesus. I pray this book will inspire readers to help fulfill Jesus' Great Commission in Matthew 28:16-20 to spread the gospel to all the nations and complete the beautiful stained-glass window that is God's family.

Made in the USA
Columbia, SC
27 April 2025

57209868R00020